1 & 2 Thessalonians

Back to the Bible Study Guides

Genesis: A God of Purpose, A People of Promise

Exodus: God's Plan, God's People

Judges: Ordinary People, Extraordinary God

Proverbs: The Pursuit of God's Wisdom

Daniel: Resolute Faith in a Hostile World

John: Face-to-Face with Jesus

Ephesians: Life in God's Family

Philippians: Maturing in the Christian Life

Hebrews: Our Superior Savior

James: Living Your Faith

Revelation: The Glorified Christ

1 & 2 THESSALONIANS

TRUSTING UNTIL
CHRIST RETURNS

WOODROW KROLL

CROSSWAY BOOKS

WHEATON, ILLINOIS

Table of Contents

How to Use This Study

The entire text of the Books of 1 & 2 Thessalonians (ESV) is included in the study. While we recommend reading the Scripture passage before you read the devotional, some have found it helpful to use the devotional as preparation for reading the Scripture. If you are unfamiliar with the English Standard Version (on which this series of studies is based), you might consider reading the included Bible selection, then the devotional, then the passage again from a different Bible translation with which you are more familiar. This will give you an excellent biblical preparation for considering the rest of the lesson.

After each devotional, there are three sections designed to help you better understand and apply the lesson's Scripture passage.

Consider It—Several questions will help you unpack and reflect on the Scripture passage of the day. These could be used for a small group discussion.

Express It—Suggestions for turning the insights from the lesson into prayer.

Go Deeper—Throughout this study, you will benefit from seeing how 1 & 2 Thessalonians fit with the rest of the Bible. This additional section will include other passages and insights from Scripture. The Go Deeper section will also allow you to consider some of the implications of the day's passage for the central theme of the study (Trusting until Christ Returns) as well as other key Scripture themes.

Trusting Jesus

The apostle Paul wrote two letters to the Macedonian city of Thessalonica. The story behind these letters involves a riot that resulted in Paul being run out of town. Why would he write letters to people who had rejected him? What happened after he left?

1 Thessalonians 1:1–10

Greeting

1 Paul, Silvanus, and Timothy,

To the church of the Thessalonians in God the Father and the Lord Jesus Christ:

Grace to you and peace.

The Thessalonians' Faith and Example

²We give thanks to God always for all of you, constantly mentioning you in our prayers, ³remembering before our God and Father your work of faith and labor of love and steadfastness of hope in our Lord Jesus Christ. ⁴For we know, brothers loved by God, that he has chosen you, ⁵because our gospel came to you not only in word, but also in power and in the Holy Spirit and with full conviction. You know what kind of men we proved to be among you for your sake. ⁶And you became imitators of us and of the Lord, for you received the word in much affliction, with the joy of the Holy Spirit, ⁷so that you became an example to all the believers in Macedonia and in Achaia. ⁸For not only has the word of the Lord sounded forth from you in Macedonia and Achaia, but your faith in God has gone forth everywhere, so that we need not say anything. ⁹For they themselves report concerning us the kind of reception we had among you, and how you turned to God from idols to serve the living and true God, ¹⁰and to wait for his Son from heaven, whom he raised from the dead, Jesus who delivers us from the wrath to come.

Key Verse

For they themselves report concerning us the kind of reception we had among you, and how you turned to God from idols to serve the living and true God (1 Thess. 1:9).

Go Deeper

After writing the two letters to Thessalonica, Paul visited there on two more occasions. The second visit was part of the westward leg of his third missionary journey (Acts 18:23–21:16). The effect of his visit was summarized by the phrase "much encouragement" (Acts 20:2). After staying in Greece three months, Paul journeyed back eastward and visited Thessalonica a third time. This time he traveled with a team made up of men from Berea, Thessalonica, Derbe, and Asia. Paul was surrounded by disciples from churches he had planted. These men would extend and expand the ministry God had given him. What a deeply satisfying journey that must have been!

Paul had already decided he would return all the way to Jerusalem but then would travel to Rome. He returned east in order to travel west. Little did he know how God would arrange for his all-expenses-paid trip to Rome, underwritten by the Roman Empire itself. Paul was eager not to let any grass grow under his sandals. He practiced what he saw in the Thessalonian believers—that they were eagerly waiting for Christ's return (1 Thess. 1:10). But he wanted to make sure that they were not sitting around waiting for that day to come! There was work to be done.

Paul actually visited Thessalonica at least three times. The city is about 200 miles north of Athens on the coastal road that travels around the Aegean Sea. His first visit, recorded in Acts 17, was part of the itinerary of Paul's second missionary journey. Although he was there for only about three weeks before trouble broke out, Paul and his team left behind a tiny group of believers. The missionaries moved on to Berea and then Athens. Somewhere along the way, Paul sent Timothy back to Thessalonica to get firsthand news on conditions there. Timothy caught up with Paul in Corinth with a glowing report about the young church and with questions they had sent for Paul to answer. Not long after that, Paul wrote the two letters we are about to study. They are, along with his letter to the Galatians, the first apostolic letters from Paul.

The news from Thessalonica encouraged Paul very much. Besides Timothy's report, other travelers Paul encountered were talking about the vibrant little church in that bustling city. Paul's purpose in writing the first letter to the Thessalonians was to deepen and clarify their unmistakable faith. They had almost immediately taken real steps in response to the Gospel, even while Paul was among them; now they needed to take further steps into the Christian life. He wanted to rejoice over their faith, commend them for how far they had come, and urge them to go on. We need the same message today. We're going to let Paul show us some of the steps that occur in the life of the believer that keep us moving on from spiritual infancy to spiritual maturity.

The place to begin is always in the beginning. And the beginning for the Christian is the step into eternal life of placing your faith in Jesus Christ as Savior. In the last two verses of the first chapter, Paul summarizes the faith story of the Thessalonian believers: "You turned to God from idols to serve the living and true God, and to wait for his Son from heaven, whom he raised from the dead, Jesus who delivers us from the wrath to come" (1 Thess. 1:9–10). Trusting Jesus always means not trusting any longer what we were trusting before. The Thessalonians turned "from idols" and "to God, to serve . . . and to wait" on Jesus.

"*The Gospel tells us we can turn from whatever we were trusting and trust Jesus instead. That's the first step in a lifetime of steps. . . . The faith walk shares the same characteristic of any journey—it begins with a step. That step is to trust Jesus.***"**

Paul looked back at the early steps of the Thessalonians, and he was thrilled. He couldn't stop thanking God (v. 2). He was delighted over the way the Gospel had come to them and changed their lives. He wrote, "Because our gospel came to you not only in word, but also in power and in the Holy Spirit and with full conviction. You know what kind of men we proved to be among you for your sake" (v. 5). Look at the "triple whammy" there. The Gospel came to them "in power," "in the Holy Spirit," and "with full conviction." When the Thessalonians received the Gospel of God, they received it not as the word of men, not as Paul's opinion and not as a particular human viewpoint. They received the Gospel, as indeed it is, as the Word of God. They did not receive it as the word of men, but they experienced it as the life-changing message that comes from God. Their response shows us the reality of God's power, the involvement of the Holy Spirit, and the creation of conviction. When Jesus described the evidence of the Holy Spirit's work in John 3:7–8, He compared it to the effects of the wind. We can't see the wind, but the moving leaves and branches catch our attention. The Thessalonians were catching people's attention because the Holy Spirit was at work in their lives beginning with their immediate response to the Gospel.

Today we are deluged by opinions. Everyone likes to express his or her viewpoint. And the often unstated rule is that one person's opinion is just as valid as another's. We've replaced truth and authority with opinion. Anytime we hear something we don't like, we set out looking for "a second opinion"! But the Gospel is not somebody's opinion. The Gospel is the story of God's love for you and for me. The Gospel is the story of how God gave His Son to die for us. And the Gospel is fact! Until we get to that Gospel, we can have all the opinions that we want—but opinions don't matter—the Gospel matters.

The Gospel tells us we can turn from whatever we were trusting and trust Jesus instead. That's the first step in a lifetime of steps. But whether the journey is short or long, the faith walk shares the same characteristic of any journey—it begins with a step. That step is to trust Jesus.

Express It

Paul began this letter with an expression of thanksgiving. Several times in correspondence he told people that he thanked God every time he thought of them. Who are the people like that in your life? Whose memory is so precious that it provokes gratitude in your heart? Take some time to express that gratitude to God, and then consider writing or calling and telling them "thank you."

Consider It

As you read 1 Thessalonians 1:1–10, consider these questions:

1) As you begin this study of 1 & 2 Thessalonians, what do you already know about these letters?

_____

_____

_____

2) As he frequently does, Paul uses the three cardinal traits (faith, hope, and love) in the opening of this letter. How does he apply them?

_____

_____

_____

3) Who were the Thessalonians imitating, and why is this important?

_____

_____

_____

4) In what ways does Paul indicate how well he remembers the difficulties of his first visit when he shared the Gospel with them?

_____

_____

_____

5) How does Paul describe the reputation of the Thessalonian church? Compare this with the city's reputation in Acts 17:10–11.

_____

_____

_____

6) Describe the tone of this opening chapter. What would have made you want to read on?

_____

_____

_____

Lesson

2

Trusting Jesus When Trials Come

It's one of the promises Jesus made that many of us don't like: "In the world you will have tribulation. But take heart; I have overcome the world" (John 16:33). So, how do we "take heart" when the trials come?

1 Thessalonians 2:1–20

Paul's Ministry to the Thessalonians

2 For you yourselves know, brothers, that our coming to you was not in vain. ²But though we had already suffered and been shamefully treated at Philippi, as you know, we had boldness in our God to declare to you the gospel of God in the midst of much conflict. ³For our appeal does not spring from error or impurity or any attempt to deceive, ⁴but just as we have been approved by God to be entrusted with the gospel, so we speak, not to please man, but to please God who tests our hearts. ⁵For we never came with words of flattery, as you know, nor with a pretext for greed—God is witness. ⁶Nor did we seek glory from people, whether from you or from others, though we could have made demands as apostles of Christ. ⁷But we were gentle among you, like a nursing mother taking care of her own children. ⁸So, being affectionately desirous of you, we were ready to share with you not only the gospel of God but also our own selves, because you had become very dear to us.

⁹For you remember, brothers, our labor and toil: we worked night and day, that we might not be a burden to any of you, while we proclaimed to you the gospel of God. ¹⁰You are witnesses, and God also, how holy and righteous and blameless was our conduct toward you believers. ¹¹For you know how, like a father with his children, ¹²we exhorted each one of you and encouraged you and charged you to walk in a manner worthy of God, who calls you into his own kingdom and glory.

¹³And we also thank God constantly for this, that when you received the word of God, which you heard from us, you accepted it not as the word of men but as what it really is, the word of God, which is at work in you believers. ¹⁴For you, brothers, became imitators of the churches of God in Christ Jesus that are in Judea. For you suffered the same things from your own countrymen as they did from the Jews, ¹⁵who killed both the Lord Jesus and the prophets, and drove us out, and displease God and oppose all mankind ¹⁶by hindering us from speaking to the Gentiles that they might be saved—so as always to fill up the measure of their sins. But God's wrath has come upon them at last!

Paul's Longing to See Them Again

¹⁷But since we were torn away from you, brothers, for a short time, in person not in heart, we endeavored the more eagerly and with great desire to see you face to face, ¹⁸because we wanted to come to you—I, Paul, again and again—but Satan hindered us. ¹⁹For what is our hope or joy or crown of boasting before our Lord Jesus at his coming? Is it not you? ²⁰For you are our glory and joy.

> # Key Verse
>
> *But though we had already suffered and been shamefully treated at Philippi, as you know, we had boldness in our God to declare to you the gospel of God in the midst of much conflict* (1 Thess. 2:2).

Go Deeper

Although the bulk of this chapter is Paul's defense of his ministry, the verses also contain an excellent profile of an effective minister of the Gospel. In creating what we could call a digital reproduction of a minister, Paul gave us a picture of an enduring servant of Christ that we can reproduce.

Every verse between 1 Thessalonians 2:3 and 2:12 contains at least one positive trait. If we want to be effective while we wait for Christ's return, we must:

Speak the gospel truthfully without impurity or manipulation (v. 3; see also Eph. 4:15).

Seek to please God and not worry about pleasing other people (v. 4; see also Gal. 1:10).

Avoid both flattery and greed in dealing with people (v. 5; see also Rom. 16:18).

Refuse to pursue "glory" from our audience or special recognition of our position (v. 6; see also 1 Cor. 9:15–16).

Practice a maternal gentleness, attentive to the needs of others (v. 7; see also 2 Tim. 2:24).

Genuinely love others to the point that we share ourselves as well as the Gospel (v. 8; see also 2 Cor. 12:15).

Work and toil, avoiding becoming an unnecessary burden on others, while sharing the Gospel (v. 9; see also 2 Thess. 3:8).

Practice holiness, righteousness, and blamelessness among believers (v. 10; see also 1 Thess. 1:5).

Treat others with a fatherly attitude (v. 11; see also Phil. 2:22).

Exhort, encourage, and challenge people to "walk in a manner worthy of God" (v. 12; see also Eph. 4:1).

Spend some time today thinking about how you can put these positive traits into practice in your life. It's the best way to serve while you await Christ's return.

When Paul talked about affliction and shameful treatment in 1 Thessalonians 2:2, he mentioned the experience he and Silas went through in Philippi shortly before their trip into Macedonia (Acts 16:11–40). His point seems to be that it would have been easy for them to be intimidated by the violent rejection of their message, but instead it emboldened them. Why? Certainly it wasn't enjoyable to be beaten or imprisoned. But Paul described their attitude as "boldness in our God" (1 Thess. 2:2). He focused not on the difficulties but on the good results that happened, even though he had been mistreated along the way. Instead of the

"When we don't know what's going to happen next, we can trust the One who does. . . . The One who died for us will be with us every step of the way. Trusting Jesus to win our battles gives us victory over the trials in our lives."

scars, he remembered the smiles on the faces of the Philippian jailer and his family during the impromptu baptismal service the night before they left town. And he still remembered the eager responses of some of the Thessalonians when they heard the Gospel for the first time.

Philippi and Thessalonica were just two of numerous hostile environments Paul faced. By the time his ministry ended, we can almost see he had two groups of followers: (1) those faithful team members who shared the load of preaching the Gospel and (2) those determined to confuse and destroy any groups of young believers. When we look back at Paul's original visit to Thessalonica, we can see a familiar pattern unfold. Paul and Silas arrived in the city knowing that there was a large enough Jewish population to support a synagogue. That's where they began their efforts because Paul felt a duty to his countrymen and because a Jewish audience already had before them God's Old Testament Word. So, we read, "And Paul went in, as was his custom, and on three Sabbath days he reasoned with them from the Scriptures, explaining and proving that it was necessary for the Christ to suffer and to rise from the dead, and saying, 'This Jesus, whom I proclaim to you, is the Christ'" (Acts 17:2–3). So far, so good.

The list of those who immediately responded to the Gospel is impressive. Some Jews and "a great many of the devout Greeks and not a few of the leading women" (Acts 17:4). The synagogue in

Thessalonica was apparently open to God-fearing Gentiles, because they heard the message and some responded.

We can see in this case, as in many cases, those who rejected the Gospel fell into two groups. Some rejected the message; others rejected the messenger. The former group included people for whom the message either seemed false or too good to be true—they were simply not ready to believe. The latter group, Luke tells us, were jealous of Paul's success and the response of people to the news about Jesus (see Acts 17:5–9). This group decided to make trouble. And Paul was forced to leave.

First Thessalonians 2:3–12 includes Paul's carefully worded response to affliction and rejection. The apostle was defending himself against criticism by the churches, by believers, and by religious leaders. It seemed as if everybody he tried to impact or affect somehow had a criticism for the apostle Paul. Questions were raised about his truthfulness (v. 3) by labeling his message an error. Some questioned Paul's motivation, accusing him of "pleasing men" to gain a following (v. 4). And there were whispers of Paul's quest for glory (v. 6). Paul felt he had to defend himself against unjust criticism, but he resisted the temptation to retaliate with criticism. He could have lashed out at all the people who had unjustly attacked him, but he didn't. He simply stated a defense of his message, his motivation, and his methods. He asked them to think back on their experience with him. Did the accusations and questions match their memory of his ministry among them? Of course not! He hadn't claimed status as an apostle but had served them as a caring father. Here was a man unjustly criticized while waiting for the return of the Lord and pointing others to Him. Paul was trusting Jesus to enable him to be earnest and steadfast and blameless and to have victory over his immediate trials.

Paul is a good example for us. In verse 14, he shifted attention to the Thessalonians and pointed to their experience of suffering for Christ. He was proud of them for their outlook toward Christ's return and their endurance under present difficulties. This kind of bold living was rooted in God, not their own strength (see v. 2). They were allowing trials to strengthen their connection with Christ.

The greatest affliction we face at this point in our lives may be the affliction of personal apprehension: fears of the unknown, fears of sickness, of war, of terrorism. Some believers today face the reality that fear is their major emotional experience. But all of us have to trust Jesus for the next step. When we don't know what's going to happen next, we can trust the One who does. When we can't *trace His hand,* we can trust His heart. The One who died for us will be with us every step of the way. Trusting Jesus to win our battles gives us victory over the trials in our lives.

Express It

As you pray, review the nature of the "troubles" in your life right now. For each item that comes to mind, ask God to help you trust Him with knowing how to bring good and His glory out of that situation. Remember that the alternative to trust isn't pretty or positive. Depending on the level of difficulty in your trouble, you may well want to ask God "if the cup can pass from you"; but if you pray that way, make sure that you follow the rest of Jesus' example and say, "Yet not what I will, but what you will" (see Mark 14:32–36).

Consider It

As you read 1 Thessalonians 2:1–20, consider these questions:

1) How would you explain the phrase "boldness in our God" (v. 2)?

_____

_____

_____

2) In what situations have you exercised boldness in God?

_____

_____

_____

3) How have you experienced the way trials can test and strengthen trust?

_____

_____

_____

4) Why do you think it is easier to doubt during difficult times?

_____

_____

_____

5) When have you experienced a sense of victory as a result of trusting Christ?

_____

_____

_____

6) When others attacked Paul's motivation, message, and methods, how did he respond to each of those attacks?

_____

_____

_____

7) How does this chapter reinforce or change your strategy for responding to trials while you wait for Christ's return?

_____

_____

_____

Trusting Jesus with Loving Relationships

The relationships we have with one another can be among the strongest sustaining gifts God gives to us for the in-between time—the time between our introduction to Jesus and that wonderful day we see Him face-to-face.

1 Thessalonians 3:1–13

3 Therefore when we could bear it no longer, we were willing to be left behind at Athens alone, ²and we sent Timothy, our brother and God's coworker in the gospel of Christ, to establish and exhort you in your faith, ³that no one be moved by these afflictions. For you yourselves know that we are destined for this. ⁴For when we were with you, we kept telling you beforehand that we were to suffer affliction, just as it has come to pass, and just as you know. ⁵For this reason, when I could bear it no longer, I sent to learn about your faith, for fear that somehow the tempter had tempted you and our labor would be in vain.

Timothy's Encouraging Report

⁶But now that Timothy has come to us from you, and has brought us the good news of your faith and love and reported that you always remember us kindly and long to see us, as we long to see you—⁷for this reason, brothers, in all our distress and affliction we have been comforted about you through your faith. ⁸For now we live, if you are standing fast in the Lord. ⁹For what thanksgiving can

---

Key Verse

And may the Lord make you increase and abound in love for one another and for all, as we do for you (1 Thess. 3:12).

---

we return to God for you, for all the joy that we feel for your sake before our God, ¹⁰as we pray most earnestly night and day that we may see you face to face and supply what is lacking in your faith?

¹¹Now may our God and Father himself, and our Lord Jesus, direct our way to you, ¹²and may the Lord make you increase and abound in love for one another and for all, as we do for you, ¹³so that he may establish your hearts blameless in holiness before our God and Father, at the coming of our Lord Jesus with all his saints.

Go Deeper

God doesn't ask us to be sinless, but He does ask us to be blameless. Paul refers to this three times in this letter: 2:10, 3:13, and 5:23. It's sometimes hard showing love to other people, isn't it? But our love is to be blamelessly holy love, because the love we show may be the only love our neighbor encounters.

We don't love that way naturally. But Paul tells us, "If possible, so far as it depends on you, live peaceably with all" (Rom. 12:18).

The New Testament uses six different Greek words to challenge us to be "blameless." Looking at those words

(continued)

Go Deeper Continued . . .

helps us understand what "blameless" means:

First—*amemptos* (1 Thess. 3:13; Phil. 2:14–15). God wants us to be faultless the moment Jesus Christ comes back. And since He could come back at any time, it's important that we keep our hands clean and our hearts pure all the time.

Second—*amomos* (Col. 1:21–23). It means to be without rebuke or without blemish; there are no chinks in your armor.

Third—*anegkletos* (Col. 1:21–23; 1 Cor. 1:8; 1 Tim. 3:10; Titus 1:6–7). It simply means that no one can call you into account. You are unaccused.

Fourth—*amiantos* (James 1:27; 1 John 1:9). This word means to be unsoiled, to be free from anything that is debased at all.

Fifth—*amometos* (2 Peter 3:14). It means that which cannot be censured.

Sixth—*anepileptos* (1 Tim. 3:2; 6:14). The word implies one not open to censure, irreproachable. Nobody can call you into account for anything. You have no skeletons in your closet.

Among many conclusions we could come to based on these verses, here are some crucial ones:

While we cannot be sinless—not this side of glory at least—we can be blameless.

God doesn't save us and get us out of hell so that we can live like we're still there. God's plan for us is that we all be blameless (1 Cor. 1:7–8; Eph. 1:4).

To be blameless will require spiritual vigilance and a significant amount of diligence (2 Pet. 3:14).

Jesus will one day present us to the Father as His treasured vessels, cleansed and undeserving of any censure (Jude 1:24).

Blameless living is the lifestyle of every Christian who truly anticipates the Lord's return. "See what kind of love the Father has given to us, that we should be called children of God; and so we are. The reason why the world does not know us is that it did not know him. Beloved, we are God's children now, and what we will be has not yet appeared; but we know that when he appears we shall be like him, because we shall see him as he is. And everyone who thus hopes in him purifies himself as he is pure" (1 John 3:1–3).

I t is somehow comforting to remember that the apostle Paul was human. He was a spiritual giant with healthy Achilles' heels. He wrote 25 percent of the New Testament, but he understood he was neither the source nor the author of the message he wrote. And alongside the message from God that he delivered to us, he also gave us plenty of glimpses of his human shortcomings and struggles.

Chapter 3 of 1 Thessalonians is an admission of personal struggle leading up to a powerful prayer. When we take those first few steps into spiritual maturity, one of our early discoveries is that there are other people traveling on the road with us. And not all of them are as nice as we are! The net of the Gospel gets thrown into our corner of the ocean, and we get pulled in with all kinds of other fish. And then the Lord informs us that not only are we going to have to learn to live together, but we're also going to have to love one another.

Sooner, rather than later, trusting Jesus for the next step between here and eternity will mean learning to trust Him for loving relationships as we all grow together. For Paul, thoughts about the fledgling church he had left in Thessalonica were filled with concern. The man who later wrote, "Do not be anxious about anything" (Phil. 4:6), knew what it was like to be anxious about something. He was very candid with his Thessalonian friends about his concern, "For this reason, when I could bear it no longer, I sent to learn about your faith, for fear that somehow the tempter had tempted you and our labor would be in vain" (1 Thess. 3:5). He didn't just stew and worry, he sent Timothy to check on the condition of their faith.

Verses 6 through 10 describe Paul's reaction to Timothy's glowing report. Paul's worst fears had been replaced by gratitude, joy, and a renewed desire to be with the Thessalonians again to "supply what [was] lacking in [their] faith" (v. 10). Timothy's description of the church featured two main traits: faith and love. For Paul, it couldn't get much better than that. They were taking the immediate steps needed as they were waiting for Christ's return.

Timothy's report sharpened the focus of Paul's prayers for his Thessalonian brethren. Verses 11–13 contain a delightful benediction, a call for God's blessing, for Paul's own next step and for an ever-increasing outpouring of love among those believers: "Now may our God . . . direct our way to you, and may the Lord make you increase and abound in love for one another and for all." This is a picture of Christians growing and overflowing with love for each other. Paul was making the point in prayer that once we have trusted

"One of the great things that can happen to us next weekend is increasing in our love for the one sitting right next to us in church. . . . Our love can increase. God wants to increase it. Part of trusting Jesus is taking the risk to love someone a little more, and after that a little more, until it's more love than we could ever imagine or come up with on our own."

Christ as Savior, a primary evidence of our salvation is always our love for God and for others. They'll "know that you are my disciples," Jesus said, "if you have love for one another" (see John 13:35). Love is a cornerstone of a life growing in grace.

One of the great things that can happen to us next weekend is increasing in our love for the one sitting right next to us in church. Now, maybe that person is a stranger or someone we've known for years. Our love can increase. God wants to increase it. Part of trusting Jesus is taking the risk to love someone a little more, and after that a little more, until it's more love than we could ever imagine or come up with on our own.

The early Christians stood out in society in two ways: (1) the purity of their lives and (2) the depth and breadth of their love. Their example challenges us today almost like a slap in the face. Wouldn't it be true to say that Christians today are often ridiculed for their lack of purity and love? Celsus, one of the early vocal critics of Christianity, lived during the second century A.D. He wrote a little book called *True Discourse,* which was anything but true. In that book, Celsus recorded what he must have thought was a Christian weak point worthy of derision: "These Christians love each other even before they get acquainted," he mocked. What he saw as weakness, we see as strength. Loving others when we barely know them is a mark of genuine spiritual life!

If you have only known a snuggly, little Christian community in your hometown all your life, get out and see the world. Discover Christians from another country, from another culture, from another ethnic background, from another denomination; you will discover that when you meet Christians who love the Lord, you are immediately attracted to one another. Sometimes the spiritual attraction will start before you are even acquainted!

Trusting Jesus means taking the step to let Him increase our loving relationships, not only with other believers but also with all (1 Thess. 3:12). How willing are you to take that step?

Express It

Praying about love may seem like an easy thing, but it isn't. When we ask God for an increased capacity for a characteristic such as love, He has a predictable way of answering our prayers. He puts us in situations and brings people into our lives that will provoke growth in that area. Growing in love involves growing pains. But desire is part of this step of trust. We can count on a promise when we pray for growth in love: "For it is God who works in you, both to will and to work for his good pleasure" (Phil. 2:13).

Consider It

As you read 1 Thessalonians 3:1–13, consider these questions:

1) What makes loving other Christians hard for you?

_____

_____

2) What does Paul say about affliction in the first five verses of this chapter?

_____

_____

3) Based on his actions and feelings, what was Paul's relationship to his new friends in Thessalonica?

_____

_____

4) Who is the "tempter" Paul mentioned in verse 5, and how might the tempter use the situation in Thessalonica to his advantage?

_____

_____

5) How did Paul describe the personal affect Timothy's report had on him? How do you identify with those feelings?

_____

_____

6) What are the basic characteristics in the life of a person who is growing spiritually?

_____

_____

7) How can love continue to grow no matter how large it has become?

_____

_____

Trusting Jesus in Immoral Times

Thessalonica was a port city, home for many cultures and worldviews. The people who first turned to Christ brought with them a background of confused morality at best or blatant immorality at worst. Trusting Jesus involved settling the issue of how much their past would influence their lives in the future. Doesn't that sound like us?

1 Thessalonians 4:1–12

A Life Pleasing to God

4 Finally, then, brothers, we ask and urge you in the Lord Jesus, that as you received from us how you ought to walk and to please God, just as you are doing, that you do so more and more. ²For you know what instructions we gave you through the Lord Jesus. ³For this is the will of God, your sanctification: that you abstain from sexual immorality; ⁴that each one of you know how to control his own body in holiness and honor, ⁵not in the passion of lust like the Gentiles who do not know God; ⁶that no one transgress and wrong his brother in this matter, because the Lord is an avenger in all these things, as we told you beforehand and solemnly warned you. ⁷For God has not called us for impurity, but in holiness. ⁸Therefore whoever disregards this, disregards not man but God, who gives his Holy Spirit to you.

> ## Key Verse
>
> *For this is the will of God, your sanctification: that you abstain from sexual immorality* (1 Thess. 4:3).

⁹Now concerning brotherly love you have no need for anyone to write to you, for you yourselves have been taught by God to love one another, ¹⁰for that indeed is what you are doing to all the brothers throughout Macedonia. But we urge you, brothers, to do this more and more, ¹¹and to aspire to live quietly, and to mind your own affairs, and to work with your hands, as we instructed you, ¹²so that you may walk properly before outsiders and be dependent on no one.

Go Deeper

How do we please God? Paul reminded the Thessalonians that his ongoing theme for them hadn't changed with this letter. He had urged them during his visit to live to please God. In this letter, that was still his primary objective (1 Thess. 4;1). In the language of this section, it is clear that we please God when we agree with His plans for us and pursue sanctification and holiness with His help (vv. 3, 7). What we must settle in our hearts and minds is God's passionate desire for our good. He does not ask from us anything that isn't for our benefit. We please God most when we desire what He desires, when we ask for His will even though our

will may be different—as Jesus prayed in the Garden of Gethsemane (Mark 14:36).

Throughout Scripture, we find numerous insights regarding this task to please God. Jesus pointed out that His life was about saying and doing what pleased His Father (see John 5:30; 8:29). In Romans 12:1, Paul tells us, "I appeal to you therefore, brothers, by the mercies of God, to present your bodies as a living sacrifice, holy and acceptable to God, which is your spiritual worship." That word *spiritual* implies a logical, expected lifestyle for each believer, and *acceptable* can also be translated "pleasing." Living

(continued)

for Christ has the same effect on God as did some of the Old Testament worship, where God is said to have "smelled the pleasing aroma" (Gen. 8:21). Both Ephesians 5:10 and Colossians 1:10 parallel the counsel of 1 Thessalonians, urging believers to watch for what pleases God and then live that way.

Pleasing God is a life-result. It's a big enough idea to take up our lives every day. Or, to put it another way, everything we do can be shaped by this central question: "Will this please God or not?" One of the central statements in all of Scripture that describes our relationship with God uses this theme of God's pleasure as the focus: "And without faith it is impossible to please him, for whoever would draw near to God must believe that he exists and that he rewards those who seek him" (Heb. 11:6). Living for Christ means that we continue to seek God's will and pleasure even after we have found Him.

The apostle Paul couldn't help but think that his friends back in Thessalonica were a small band of brothers and sisters in a hostile world. They were terribly outnumbered. And the hostility of the world would become harsher when those young Christians began to practice a lifestyle distinct from what was typical in that pagan environment. Paul wanted to instruct and encourage them. He knew they needed to move from that one simple step of faith in Christ to multiple steps of a life in Christ. We need to do the same.

How do we do that? In the first verse of chapter 4, Paul tells his friends, "It's time to grow up." This isn't new teaching but a directive Paul had already given them, "that as you received from us how you ought to live and to please God, just as you are doing, that you do so more and more" (1 Thess. 4:1). Paul is basically saying, "I've heard good news about how you are doing. That's great! Now, keep doing it even more!"

For Paul, living the Christian life was like walking a step at a time with a destination in mind. He told the Ephesians, "I therefore, a prisoner for the Lord, urge you to walk in a manner worthy of the calling to which you have been called" (Eph. 4:1).

Not only is it by faith that we were saved (see Eph. 2:8), it's also by faith that we live (see Col. 2:6–7). The faith that brought us to new

❝Now, *trusting Jesus as we live in an immoral world means that we have to practice contentment with what Jesus gives us. And when we live in contentment with what Jesus gives us, we have found success in life.***❞**

life in Christ Jesus is the same kind of faith that carries us on to full maturity in Christ Jesus. It's by this faith that we walk and live in ways that please the One who loved us, which is our purpose (see 1 Thess. 4:1 again).

If we are walking and living with Christ, we should regularly monitor our decisions with the prayer, "Lord, is what I'm doing pleasing You?" because when we enter eternity we want the Lord to say, "Well done, good and faithful servant." But that requires periodic checkups along the way. We need to keep short accounts with Him.

Notice how verses 3 and 7 act as parentheses around some specific behavior patterns. Before and after Paul talks about our conduct, he talks about God's desires for us. "For this is the will of God, your sanctification. . . . For God has not called us for impurity, but in holiness" (vv. 3, 7). When God puts limits on our behavior, He always does so for our good. When we trust Jesus, we have to walk in such a way that we avoid impurity. And listen: that is a non-negotiable in the Christian life. God doesn't accept sexual impurity one time; He doesn't accept it ever—because He has our best interests at heart.

The specifics in this case are spelled out in three phrases that begin the same way: "that you abstain from sexual immorality" (v. 3); "that each one of you know how to control his own body" (v. 4); and "that no one transgress and wrong his brother in this matter" (v. 6). Paul says we have to learn how to control our passions. We trust Jesus to help us to learn how to control our drives, our sexual cravings, our bodies, and our treatment of others. Walking with Jesus always involves living in a way that respects God and others.

The holiness God expects to help us develop doesn't involve isolation from the world but constant righteous interaction with the world. It often seems as if the Church today is afraid of holiness. Perhaps that's because we don't have a clue what holiness is.

One way to describe holiness can be found in the positive encouragement Paul gives his friends in verses 9–12. These directions parallel the constraints of the previous paragraph. Holiness is expressed through loving one another (v. 9). To this central objective, Paul added that they should seek: "to do this [love] more and more" (v. 10), "to aspire to live quietly" (v. 11), "to mind [their] own affairs" (v. 11) and "to work with [their] hands" (v. 11). It turns out that a quiet, thoughtful kind of life pleases the Lord God— not constantly badgering those around us, not constantly borrowing from other people but being content with what God gives us.

Now, trusting Jesus as we live in an immoral world means that we have to practice contentment with what Jesus gives us. And when we live in contentment with what Jesus gives us, we have found success in life. Trusting Jesus this way is how we can maintain that distinction He was talking about when He said that His disciples would be in the world but not of the world (see John 15:19).

Express It

Life is a continual cascade of choices. But at any time most of us face a handful of decisions we know will affect our lives for a long time. What are those decisions for you? How willing are you to pursue God's pleasure and hold each of those choices up to the light of the question, "Which alternative fits best with God's purpose of creating sanctification and holiness in my life?" Use that question to pray through your current set of pressing choices. Experience God's pleasure by determining to do His will.

Consider It

As you read 1 Thessalonians 4:1–12, consider these questions:

1) What previous teaching was Paul reinforcing in this letter?

_____

_____

2) How did Paul compare God's behavioral expectations with the standards of the pagan world?

_____

_____

3) This section speaks about God's desire for your sanctification and holiness. How would you describe a lifestyle that exhibits holiness?

_____

_____

4) According to v. 8, when a person deliberately rejects the previous behavioral guidelines, who is he or she rejecting? Why does Paul make this a crucial part of his teaching?

_____

_____

5) What is a person who claims to be a Christian but insists on living an immoral life failing to understand?

_____

_____

6) What about the positive pursuits listed in vv. 11–12 appeals to you? Why?

_____

_____

7) In what areas of your life do you know you need to step more deliberately toward holiness?

_____

_____

Trusting Jesus about the Future

The part of the Good News that announces Jesus' return can create some confusion. We're challenged to have an open-ended expectation. He could return at any moment. But we want to know the date. We think it would be easier to live faithfully if we knew God's schedule. Would it?

1 Thessalonians 4:13–5:11

The Coming of the Lord

¹³But we do not want you to be uninformed, brothers, about those who are asleep, that you may not grieve as others do who have no hope. ¹⁴For since we believe that Jesus died and rose again, even so, through Jesus, God will bring with him those who have fallen asleep. ¹⁵For this we declare to you by a word from the Lord, that we who are alive, who are left until the coming of the Lord, will not precede those who have fallen asleep. ¹⁶For the Lord himself will descend from heaven with a cry of command, with the voice of an archangel, and with the sound of the trumpet of God. And the dead in Christ will rise first. ¹⁷Then we who are alive, who are left, will be caught up together with them in the clouds to meet the Lord in the air, and so we will always be with the Lord. ¹⁸Therefore encourage one another with these words.

The Day of the Lord

5 Now concerning the times and the seasons, brothers, you have no need to have anything written to you. ²For you yourselves are fully aware that the day of the Lord will come like a thief in the night. ³While people are saying, "There is peace and security," then sudden destruction will come upon them as labor pains come upon a pregnant

> # Key Verse
>
> *"For since we believe that Jesus died and rose again, even so, through Jesus, God will bring with him those who have fallen asleep"* (1 Thess. 4:14).

you are not in darkness, brothers, for that day to surprise you like a thief. ⁵For you are all children of light, children of the day. We are not of the night or of the darkness. ⁶So then let us not sleep, as others do, but let us keep awake and be sober. ⁷For those who sleep, sleep at night, and those who get drunk, are drunk at night. ⁸But since we belong to the day, let us be sober, having put on the breastplate of faith and love, and for a helmet the hope of salvation. ⁹For God has not destined us for wrath, but to obtain salvation through our Lord Jesus Christ, ¹⁰who died for us so that whether we are awake or asleep we might live with him. ¹¹Therefore encourage one another and build one another up, just as you are doing.

Go Deeper

This lesson's passage and a parallel passage in 1 Corinthians 15 explain important details about the stages of Christ's return. Paul calls this area of teaching "a mystery" (1 Cor. 15:51). Much we will not understand now, but we can trust God to do what He says He will do. God unveiled through Paul information about His eternal plan that had been kept hidden until then. Ponder that information.

(continued)

Go Deeper Continued . . .

Begin by reading 1 Corinthians 15:51–58. The wonder and mystery is that not all of us are going to die. The same thing he wrote in 1 Thessalonians 4 he also wrote later in 1 Corinthians 15. We need to trust Jesus for the future. And if our next step is the step into glory at the Rapture, we can depend on Him to meet us in the air. He's been through enemy territory before. Remember, Satan is the prince of the power of the air (see Eph. 2:2). When we get caught up to glory, we're going through enemy territory, but we can count on our Commander-in-Chief to lead the way safely and rather dramatically. That's why it's significant that He Himself will descend, and He will shout (1 Thess. 4:16). Taking us to heaven is too important to the Lord Jesus to assign this task to one of His angel-lieutenants.

These passages don't deal with Christ's final return. This is not Jesus coming to establish His kingdom on the earth. This passage is very different from Revelation 19, when Jesus comes again. In 1 Thessalonians 4, Christ comes in the clouds. In Revelation 19, Christ comes to the earth. In 1 Thessalonians 4, Christ comes alone. In Revelation 19, Christ comes with an army. In 1 Thessalonians 4, Christ comes for His saints. In Revelation 19, Christ comes with His saints. In 1 Thessalonians 4, Christ comes on a retrieval mission. In Revelation 19, Christ comes on a battle mission. In 1 Thessalonians 4, Satan and Antichrist don't even appear. In Revelation 19, they are central characters in the story. The passage in 1 Thessalonians is truly a great source of comfort for those who are walking with Christ. Let it be a source of comfort to you. You'll see your loved ones "in Christ" again. That's God's promise to you.

This section of Paul's letter is probably an ongoing response to the issues and questions Timothy reported after his visit. In the excitement of the early days of their faith, the Thessalonians were anticipating Christ's imminent return. They thought He would be back any day for them. Then some of the believers began to die. What was God's plan for them? Troubled hearts wanted to know.

When Paul writes about falling asleep in 1 Thessalonians 4:13–15, it's evident from the context he's not talking about a nap; he is talking about people who have died. Using the word *sleep* as a metaphor for death is a common practice in Scripture. His point is, "I don't want you to be [uninformed] about those who have died already." The information Paul was about to reveal to them would allow them to sorrow with hope rather than "grieve as others do who have no hope" (4:13). If we're going to trust Jesus for the final step in

> *"For a follower of Jesus, life and death must be seen from eternity's point of view. Even the best fleeting pleasures in this world are not worth exchanging for our souls. . . . We follow the Lord Jesus Christ, "who died for us so that whether we are awake or asleep we might live with him."*

our lives, the step into the future, we have to trust Him that perhaps that step will come for us by resurrection after we have died. Verse 14 clearly spells out our basis for hope when it comes to our own death: "For since we believe that Jesus died and rose again, even so, through Jesus, God will bring with him those who have fallen asleep" (4:14).

So, we have the hope of resurrection. We know that there is going to be a tomorrow. And that tomorrow is absolutely secure and sure for us because of Jesus' resurrection from the dead. Even if we die, we have God's promise we will live again. Jesus said, "Because I live, you also will live" (John 14:19). That's His promise to you; you can believe it.

Now, why should we not grieve like others who have no hope? First, because we have here a promise from God's Word that gives us hope. Second, we have a glorious future with the Lord Jesus. Jesus also has assured us that because He lives, we shall live also (see also John 11:25–26).

We don't have to be worried about dying even though we don't like the prospect of it. If we are in Christ, we know that we have a hope of resurrection. But let's not lose sight of something even better than that! "For this we declare to you by a word from the Lord, *that we who are alive, who are left until the coming of the Lord,* will not precede those who have fallen asleep" (1 Thess. 4:15, italics added). There's something exhilarating (and comforting) about the possibility of cheating death!

Paul's teaching is clear. Some who follow Christ will die before our Lord returns for us. Those who die before Christ returns are not doomed. Christ will raise the bodies of those who have trusted Him as Savior but have died, and their bodies will be reunited with their spirits that went to live with the Lord at their death. Thus, those dead will be just as alive at Christ's return as those of us who have never died. Together we will be caught up into the air to meet the Lord. Talk about a promise of victory!

But how do we know that? Here's what the Bible says: "For the Lord himself will descend from heaven with a cry of command, with the voice of an archangel, and with the sound of the trumpet of God. And the dead in Christ will rise first" (4:16). Let's think about the sequence here. First, the Lord descends from heaven with a shout—a commanding shout. We've seen this before. When Jesus raised Lazarus from the dead, "He cried out with a loud voice, 'Lazarus, come out'" (John 11:43). There is precedent for Jesus shouting, "Come on up here!" and waking the dead. This passage also mentions the trumpet of God and the voice of the archangel. We know from Scripture (see Matt. 24:29–31; 1 Cor. 15:51–58) that these are appropriate accompanying sounds to the mighty voice of Christ. What a wake-up call!

Next, 1 Thessalonians 4:17 tells us that after the dead in Christ rise from their graves into the air, then God's living saints will join them on the way up to heaven. This is definitely a one-of-a-kind experience awaiting believers. The word for "caught up" has an exciting aspect to it that is best captured in a term borrowed from the Latin translation of the Bible—*Rapture*. We may not know all the details, but we know the Rapture is God's catching us up to live forever with Him in heaven (see also Acts 1:8–9). The very word used for Jesus ascending into heaven when He left this earth is the same word that is used for our ascending into heaven when He catches us up to be with Him forever (1 Thess. 4:17).

The first eleven verses of 1 Thessalonians 5 bring the subject back to the present. Once we've settled the issue of death, we need to get busy with the issues of living for Christ on this side of eternity.

Paul points to the *sleepwalking* tendency of people in this world. Their ultimate goal is peace and security in this life. For a follower of Jesus, life and death must be seen from eternity's point of view. Even the best fleeting pleasures in this world are not worth exchanging for our souls (see Mark 8:36). We follow the Lord Jesus Christ, "who died for us so that whether we are awake or asleep we might live with him" (1 Thess. 5:10).

Express It

If you haven't experienced grief before, it is highly likely that you will at some time in the future. Pain and loss are not easy. They are part of living in a fallen world. But these verses give us hope and comfort. If you are grieving right now, ask God for a renewed sense of the security you and your loved ones can have in Him. Leave tomorrow in His hands and live for Him today.

Consider It

As you read 1 Thessalonians 4:13–5:11, consider these questions:

1) Where did Paul say his teaching on the fate of the dead came from? (See 1 Thess. 4:15.)

_____

_____

2) What is the difference between grieving with hope and grieving without hope?

_____

_____

3) In both 4:18 and 5:11 Paul tells us this teaching can encourage us. What does he mean?

_____

_____

4) How has the promise of the resurrection and Jesus' return influenced your view of death?

_____

_____

5) What would you most like to be doing the moment you are caught up to meet Christ?

_____

_____

6) How would you begin to respond to someone who stated he or she thought life ended with physical death?

_____

_____

7) Knowing that Christ could return for us at any moment, what kind of a checklist should you mentally go through each day to make sure you are ready?

_____

_____

Trusting Jesus into the Unknown

This first letter to the Thessalonians may not have had the theological depth Paul demonstrated in later letters like Romans and Ephesians; that's partly due to his audience. He wanted to keep this letter simple and practical. He gave them what they needed to know now. He certainly gave them the basics for spiritual survival.

1 Thessalonians 5:12–28

Timothy's Encouraging Report

¹²We ask you, brothers, to respect those who labor among you and are over you in the Lord and admonish you, ¹³and to esteem them very highly in love because of their work. Be at peace among yourselves. ¹⁴And we urge you, brothers, admonish the idle, encourage the fainthearted, help the weak, be patient with them all. ¹⁵See that no one repays anyone evil for evil, but always seek to do good to one another and to everyone. ¹⁶Rejoice always, ¹⁷pray without ceasing, ¹⁸give thanks in all circumstances; for this is the will of God in Christ Jesus for you. ¹⁹Do not quench the Spirit. ²⁰Do not despise prophecies, ²¹but test everything; hold fast what is good. ²²Abstain from every form of evil.

²³Now may the God of peace himself sanctify you completely, and may your

> # Key Verse
>
> *He who calls you is faithful; he will surely do it* (1 Thess. 5:24).

whole spirit and soul and body be kept blameless at the coming of our Lord Jesus Christ. ²⁴He who calls you is faithful; he will surely do it.

²⁵Brothers, pray for us.

²⁶Greet all the brothers with a holy kiss.

²⁷I put you under oath before the Lord to have this letter read to all the brothers.

²⁸The grace of our Lord Jesus Christ be with you.

Go Deeper

When we talk about the God of peace (Rom. 15:33, 16:20; 2 Thess. 3:16), we should include at least two ways we experience this peace:
1) Peace *with* God (see Rom. 5:1) and 2) the peace *of* God (see Phil. 4:7; Col. 3:15). These prepositions become extremely important in our theological understanding. First of all, God establishes peace *with* us. He gives us peace as a commodity. He gives us peace as the joy of our lives. When we originally trusted the Lord Jesus for the step of salvation in our lives, we actually had a peace treaty signed between God and us (see Rom. 5:1). Our rebellion and war against God is over because Jesus brought the two warring parties together.

We have surrendered. We have peace *with* God. In Ephesians, Paul says, "But now in Christ Jesus you who once were far off have been brought near by the blood of Christ. For he himself is our peace, who has made us both one and has broken down in his flesh the dividing wall of hostility" (Eph. 2:13–14). Notice that Jesus doesn't just bring peace to us; He *is* our peace. He doesn't just sign the treaty between God and us; He *is* the treaty, the bond between God the Father and us.

Mentioning the God *of* peace also brings up our peace-filled relationship from God that spills (or should spill) over to everybody else. As God's Word puts it, "Do not be anxious about anything, but

(continued)

Go Deeper Continued . . .

in everything by prayer and supplication with thanksgiving let your requests be made known to God. And the peace of God, which surpasses all understanding, will guard your hearts and your minds in Christ Jesus" (Phil. 4:6–7). The same One who brought the peace treaty to us also brings daily peace to our hearts and minds. Jesus is the one we peacefully trust to give us a future that is set apart for Him in peace.

Well, we come now to the last section of 1 Thessalonians and Paul's concluding remarks. We can prepare ourselves for the rapid-fire tone of these final verses if we imagine the setting. One of the things many of Paul's traveling companions had in common is that most of them could write. In all likelihood, when we talk about Paul writing, we are generally referring to Paul dictating letters to others like Timothy and Silvanus mentioned in the opening verse of this letter. Timothy was the messenger reporting his findings in Thessalonica, so Silvanus may have been the scribe.

By the time we read 1 Thessalonians 5:11, we've reached a natural conclusion to the letter. Paul has dealt with the pressing issue of encouraging the believers in Thessalonica to persevere until the end and encourage one another along the way. Paul senses there's a little more the Lord wants him to say, so he begins to mention, one after another, practical matters about life. There are always good things worth mentioning that will help us persevere as we walk with Christ.

Paul uses the term *brothers* (or *brethren,* meaning both brothers and sisters) five times in these verses. His clipped commands are softened in tone but not in urgency. First, Paul deals with leadership issues, directing the church to maintain a high level of respect and honor for those God calls to teach and lead. His brief note, "Be at peace among yourselves" (v. 13), could be a gentle warning not to choose between leaders and create division.

Next comes a group of directives headed by the phrase "we urge you" and covering 14 different issues. These alternate between the brothers' relationship with each other and their relationship with

"Battles come into our lives. The conflicts and setbacks can unnerve us if we forget that we are never alone in our waiting, watching, and working. This life, until Christ comes, is not about self-improvement; it's about God's work in and through our lives."

God. The idle are to be admonished, the fainthearted encouraged, the weak helped and all treated with patience (see v. 14). Opportunities for revenge are to be ignored and ways to do good are to be sought (see v. 15). Rejoicing, praying, and thanksgiving are to be continuous and pervasive—because this is God's will (see vv. 16–18). The last five issues involve spiritual openness and guardedness.

Verses 23–24 record a kind of "catch-all" expression that we frequently find in Paul's writings. He fashions a benediction (a request for God's blessing) to conclude his letter. This entire book is about the coming of the Lord, the return of Jesus. Paul reminded the Thessalonians (and us) that we are waiting for Jesus to come back. And while we're waiting, we're watching. And while we're watching, we're working. And while we're working, we're improving ourselves and others in word and in deed. At any and every point, battles come into our lives. The conflicts and setbacks can unnerve us if we forget that we are never alone in our waiting, watching, and working. This life, until Christ comes, is not about self-improvement; it's about God's work in and through our lives.

Paul begins his benediction with a specific title for God, the God of peace (see Go Deeper). One of the promises Jesus left us was to provide us with a peace we can find only in Him: "Peace I leave with you; my peace I give to you. Not as the world gives do I give to you. Let not your hearts be troubled, neither let them be afraid" (John 14:27). We can trust the Lord *for* peace and trust Him for living *in* peace with others. According to 1 Thessalonians 5:23, we are also trusting God to preserve us blameless at the Lord's return. When Jesus Christ comes back, we want Him to find us with clean hands and a pure heart. We need to get in the habit of doing a daily spiritual check of our lives. The reason we can anticipate peace and blamelessness is found in the next verse: "He who calls you is faithful; he will surely do it" (v. 24).

As we step into the unknown immediate future, we can trust Jesus to guard each step. This last verse points us to two powerful reasons for trust: God's faithful Word and God's faithful character. Both our exposure to God's Word and our experience with God's character lead us to the same conclusion—He is faithful. We can reevaluate ourselves constantly, but we must reach some conclusions about God. If we let each moment and every issue that enters our lives determine our view of God, we will not have peace. Paul didn't know what the next life-step would be and neither do we. We don't know Jesus' next step for us. That's why we simply have to make the commitment to trust Him. He will surely do it—every *it* we need. He will preserve us blameless. He will be faithful in all that He does. He will bring peace to us. He will sanctify us. And He will take us all the way home because God is trustworthy!

Express It

One way to think about prayer involves realizing that we get to meet with God, in the moment, to talk about the past and the future. Confession and thanksgiving focus on the past—what we have done and what God has done for us. Requests focus on the future, entrusting our next steps to God and what He will do for us. And the worship and praise part of prayer has no time stamp because we're seeking to express our awareness of the One who IS, the I Am. Consciously include these different parts of prayer as you pray.

Consider It

As you read 1 Thessalonians 5:12–28, consider these questions:

1) All of us in the Church rely on the leadership of others. What guidelines does this passage give us in our view of spiritual leaders?

_____

_____

2) According to verses 14–18, what actions can we take, confident that we are doing God's will?

_____

_____

3) What does it mean to "quench the Spirit" (v. 19)?

_____

_____

4) Compare verses 13 and 23. How do we experience and maintain peace in the Church?

_____

_____

5) How many of the specific behavior items in these verses touched on a tender spot in your life?

_____

_____

6) What do you think it means to "rejoice always" and "pray without ceasing" (v. 16)?

_____

_____

7) What are some things you can do to keep your spirit, soul, and body blameless until Jesus comes? (See v. 23.)

_____

_____

Trusting Jesus in the Face of God's Judgment

The news media may be filled with stories of impending economic disasters, ecological meltdowns, and continual wars, but the Bible doesn't elevate any of these events beyond being possible side effects to the actual fate of the world. God has determined the final act of history.

2 Thessalonians 1:1–12

Greeting

1 Paul, Silvanus, and Timothy,

To the church of the Thessalonians in God our Father and the Lord Jesus Christ:

²Grace to you and peace from God our Father and the Lord Jesus Christ.

Thanksgiving

³We ought always to give thanks to God for you, brothers, as is right, because your faith is growing abundantly, and the love of every one of you for one another is increasing. ⁴Therefore we ourselves boast about you in the churches of God for your steadfastness and faith in all your persecutions and in the afflictions that you are enduring.

The Judgment at Christ's Coming

⁵This is evidence of the righteous judgment of God, that you may be considered worthy of the kingdom of God, for which you are also suffering— ⁶since indeed God considers it just to repay with affliction those who afflict you, ⁷and to grant relief to you who are afflicted as well as to us, when the Lord Jesus is revealed from heaven with his mighty angels ⁸in flaming fire, inflicting

> ## Key Verse
>
> *This is evidence of the righteous judgment of God, that you may be considered worthy of the kingdom of God, for which you are also suffering* (2 Thess. 1:5).

vengeance on those who do not know God and on those who do not obey the gospel of our Lord Jesus. ⁹They will suffer the punishment of eternal destruction, away from the presence of the Lord and from the glory of his might, ¹⁰when he comes on that day to be glorified in his saints, and to be marveled at among all who have believed, because our testimony to you was believed. ¹¹To this end we always pray for you, that our God may make you worthy of his calling and may fulfill every resolve for good and every work of faith by his power, ¹²so that the name of our Lord Jesus may be glorified in you, and you in him, according to the grace of our God and the Lord Jesus Christ.

Go Deeper

Revelation 19 parallels the teaching of 2 Thessalonians 1. It is also a glorious passage but difficult to teach. Notice the description of Jesus in Revelation 19:11: He "is called Faithful and True, and in righteousness he judges and makes war." Both these passages convey the awesome finality of God's judgment.

Jesus is also called "The Word of God" in Revelation 19:13. Two times in Scripture, the word *word (logos)* is used as a proper name. It is used once in Revelation 19 and again in John 1:1 where we read, "In the beginning was the Word, and the Word was with God, and the Word was God." The Word of God, Jesus,

(continued)

Go Deeper Continued . . .

is coming back to make war. He will dispense judgment. These pictures of the final times of humanity make us shudder in concern and wonder.

Daniel 7:9–10 gives us further glimpses into the stunning visual panorama of the last days (see also Isa. 66:15–16). The description of Jesus in Daniel tells us "his throne was fiery flames; its wheels were burning fire." God's activity is accompanied by fire. His judgments are like cleansing fire. In 2 Thessalonians 1:8, Jesus comes in flaming fire to take vengeance on those who do not know God and on those who do not obey the Gospel of God.

Hebrews reminds us, "It is a fearful thing to fall into the hands of the living God" (Heb. 10:31). We dare not wish God's judgment on anyone, because judging someone shows that we don't appreciate God's grace in our own lives. Our prayer ought to be that no one who knows us should be able to say, "You knew better and never told me." Ask God for a bold love for others that doesn't overlook any opportunity for witness.

P aul's second letter to the Thessalonians followed soon after the first. In 1 Thessalonians he wrote to them about the Lord gathering His Church up to Him, both the living believers and those who had died. He said that some of us may not even die because the Lord may catch us up to be with Him in the air, and that's good news! He zipped that letter off with Timothy to the Thessalonians.

When they read Paul's first letter, they said, "Oh good, Jesus is coming back so we can quit our jobs now. We can just go up the hill and wait." When Paul heard about their response, he realized they needed the rest of the story. So, he helped them (and us) to understand that there is also a time when Jesus will come back—not to gather the saints together but to come with the saints to make war and to bring judgment to this planet. Basically, what Paul had to say in 2 Thessalonians relates to that event.

Paul's second letter begins much like the first, with glowing words of encouragement for the Thessalonians. Stories of their

"We . . . will experience our share of suffering and affliction in this fallen world. But we need to trust Jesus to exercise righteous judgment on the world. If we can trust Jesus for our eternal salvation, we can trust Him to mete out to the world, which has not received that salvation, just the right amount of judgment—not too little and not too much."

faith and love were spreading. And the fact that they were growing spiritually in the face of "persecutions" and "afflictions" was all the more impressive. Paul used their hardships as a transition into his teaching about the end times. He wrote, "This is evidence" (2 Thess. 1:5) to make the point that unmerited suffering of believers is a reminder that God still holds the power for a just conclusion. God will "repay with affliction those who afflict you, and to grant relief to you who are afflicted" (vv. 6–7). The blatant injustices of this world have not been resolved, but they will be—mark God's Word.

Second Thessalonians 1:7–10 is a tough passage. But it includes teaching that God wants us to know about because it's coming, and it's certain. It's not part of our future, thank God, but it is part of the future for this world. We have been given this information for the in-between time. Like the Thessalonians, we, too, will experience our share of suffering and affliction in this fallen world. But we need to trust Jesus to exercise righteous judgment on the world.

If we can trust Jesus for our eternal salvation, we can trust Him to mete out to the world, which has not received that salvation, just the right amount of judgment—not too little and not too much. God will judge righteously based on His perfect knowledge of men's hearts and motives. So, when things we see on television or read in the newspaper trouble us, we turn them over to God's wisdom and judgment. The day is coming when the wrath of God will be revealed from heaven. And when that wrath is revealed from heaven, Jesus Christ will come riding out as King of Kings and Lord of Lords.

Verse 8 talks about Christ and His mighty angels "in flaming fire, inflicting vengeance." Now, flaming fire is often used in the Bible as a visual evidence of God's presence (see Exodus 3). According to this verse, there are two categories of individuals on whom this judgment will fall: (1) those who do not know God and (2) those who do not obey the Gospel of our Lord Jesus. Those who do not know God are people who are willfully ignorant of God. The key word there is *willfully* (see also Rom. 1:21–23). It's not that they don't know that God exists; they refuse to accept knowing that God exists. That's the first group.

The second group is those who know but are willfully disobedient. They are those who say, "Well, sure, I know God exists; I've read about it. I went to Sunday school as a kid, you know. And I decided that He didn't ever do anything for me. So, I'm not going to do anything for Him." But they are wrong—Christ did everything for them. Rejecting Him means their fate is sealed (see John 3:36).

According to 2 Thessalonians 1:9, horrible judgment will come. We must not forget what makes hell *hell.* It's the fact that God isn't there. God is omnipresent, but when we leave the intimate presence of God, it is hell. Hell will ultimately involve spending eternity outside of the intimate presence of God.

But verse 10 follows with a bright ray of hope. Non-believers can claim an opportunity to believe even as they are reading about the fate that otherwise awaits them. When Christ comes, He will be "marveled at among all who have believed, because our testimony to you was believed" (v. 10). There are some people who say, "I don't want to have anything to do with God"; and then we give them our testimony and, lo and behold, they are saved by the grace of God. That's why it's so important that we are consistent in our witness to others and consistent in the way we live for the Lord God—if our friends don't trust the Lord as Savior, they must meet the Lord as judge.

Express It

Pray for those you know who do not know the Savior. Let their faces appear in your mind. Think of the danger before them if they should step into eternity without Christ or face His return without salvation. Ask God for both guidance and courage as you relate to them. We cannot decide for them, but we may be a part of God's plan to reach them before it's too late.

Consider It

As you read 2 Thessalonians 1:1–12, consider these questions:

1) What were Paul's specific compliments for the church in Thessalonica?

2) According to vv. 5–7, what are the by-products of being worthy of the kingdom of God?

3) How does Paul later use the term *worthy* in v. 11?

4) Why do you think it is difficult for us to accept the harshness and finality of God's judgment?

5) Why is it crucial to remember that God does both the saving and the judging, not us?

6) How often do you ask God to allow both your good and bad experiences to be used to bring other people to Him? In what ways have you seen Him answer?

7) What details does Paul give us in vv. 11–12 about his prayers for the Thessalonian believers?

Trusting Jesus in the Long Days of Waiting

Are we there yet? Is it time yet? Is He here yet? Waiting is agony for children. As we get older, waiting isn't much easier. We have a hard time living in a state of perpetual anticipation. The Day of the Lord is coming! How are we to wait?

2 Thessalonians 2:1–17

The Man of Lawlessness

2 Now concerning the coming of our Lord Jesus Christ and our being gathered together to him, we ask you, brothers, [2]not to be quickly shaken in mind or alarmed, either by a spirit or a spoken word, or a letter seeming to be from us, to the effect that the day of the Lord has come. [3]Let no one deceive you in any way. For that day will not come, unless the rebellion comes first, and the man of lawlessness is revealed, the son of destruction, [4]who opposes and exalts himself against every so-called god or object of worship, so that he takes his seat in the temple of God, proclaiming himself to be God. [5]Do you not remember that when I was still with you I told you these things? [6]And you know what is restraining him now so that he may be revealed in his time. [7]For the mystery of lawlessness is already at work. Only he who now restrains it will do so until he is out of the way. [8]And then the lawless one will be revealed, whom the Lord Jesus will kill with the breath of his mouth and bring to nothing by the appearance of his coming. [9]The coming of the lawless one is by the activity of Satan with all power and false signs and wonders, [10]and with all wicked deception for those who are perishing, because they refused to love the truth and so be saved. [11]Therefore God sends them a strong delusion, so that they may believe what is false, [12]in order that all may be condemned who did not believe the truth but had pleasure in unrighteousness.

> # Key Verse
>
> *Now concerning the coming of our Lord Jesus Christ and our being gathered together to him, we ask you, brothers, not to be quickly shaken in mind or alarmed, either by a spirit or a spoken word, or a letter seeming to be from us, to the effect that the day of the Lord has come* (2 Thess. 2:1–2).

Stand Firm

[13]But we ought always to give thanks to God for you, brothers beloved by the Lord, because God chose you as the firstfruits to be saved, through sanctification by the Spirit and belief in the truth. [14]To this he called you through our gospel, so that you may obtain the glory of our Lord Jesus Christ. [15]So then, brothers, stand firm and hold to the traditions that you were taught by us, either by our spoken word or by our letter.

[16]Now may our Lord Jesus Christ himself, and God our Father, who loved us and gave us eternal comfort and good hope through grace, [17]comfort your hearts and establish them in every good work and word.

Go Deeper

The "day of the Lord" is an expression used throughout the Bible. There is a period of future history, frequently mentioned in the Old Testament, when God will bring final judgment on this earth. That's the day of the Lord. And

(continued)

Go Deeper Continued . . .

while the phrase "day of the Lord" is used in a variety of settings, it is generally used as a way to talk about God's judging the earth. Here are some examples: (1) Isaiah 13:6, 9 refers to the day of the Lord as a day of destruction; (2) Jeremiah 46:10 explains the day of the Lord as the day of vengeance; and (3) Zephaniah 1:14–15 has multiple descriptive words for the day of the Lord—"The great day of the LORD is near, near and hastening fast; the sound of the day of the LORD is bitter; the mighty man cries aloud there. A day of wrath is that day, a day of distress and anguish, a day of ruin and devastation, a day of darkness and gloom, a day of clouds and thick darkness" (Zeph. 1:14–15). It is not a pretty picture. All the way through the Old Testament, the day of the Lord is depicted for us as a day when God gets His holy, righteous due on a world that has sinned against Him.

The New Testament picks up this theme and sharpens it. While the exact phrase is not used, the entire Book of Revelation, which is actually titled "The Revelation of Jesus Christ," is about the day of the Lord and surrounding events. Other references can be found in Acts 2:20; 1 Corinthians 5:5; 2 Corinthians 1:14; 1 Thessalonians 5:2; and 2 Peter 3:10.

We need to remember that day is coming! We don't know the exact day on the calendar, but it is coming. God has promised it will come. The world hasn't seen anything like this yet. And if we are in Christ, we will be with Christ and ride out of heaven with Him on that day!

The first chapter of 2 Thessalonians summarizes the world's last days. Now, this second chapter steps back to today. Not only do we trust Jesus for the final step in history, but we also have to trust Jesus for the next step in waiting before that event occurs. God's Word allows us to wait as informed *waiters*. The Bible gives us plenty to do while we wait. In fact, our waiting shouldn't look that much like waiting to the watching world. Remember, Noah was waiting for the flood and busy building the ark at the same time. Which action got people's attention?

Paul begins the second chapter talking about "our Lord Jesus Christ and our being gathered together to him" (2 Thess. 2:1). This is not the final step of the last chapter; this is the family step of the dead and living in Christ meeting Him in the air. But when he

> **❝***Not only do we trust Jesus for the final step in history, but we also have to trust Jesus for the next step in waiting before that event occurs.*❞

immediately mentioned "the day of the Lord" in verse 2, he was again referring to the final step (see Go Deeper). To paraphrase, he says, "Now, remember what I said about the Rapture? Don't believe all you have to look forward to is the day of Lord." They had a problem. One of the things people begin to struggle with when they have waited for a while is the nagging feeling they missed the event. The Thessalonians thought perhaps they had missed the Rapture. They thought Jesus had already come and left them behind, and now they were facing the Judgment Day of the Lord. Paul wrote, "Wrong, friends! You are confusing these events! See, there are some things that have to happen before that day comes, and they haven't happened. So, don't worry! You haven't missed it!" He didn't want them to be "deceived" into disappointment.

Paul's case is simple: "For that day will not come [the Day of the Lord will not come], unless the rebellion comes first" (v. 3). Other things have to happen before anyone can say, "Ah ha, the day of the Lord is getting close." Now, there were people in the Old Testament who thought that the day of the Lord was at hand. And, quite frankly, we may think exactly the same way today. How can God not bring judgment to this earth? Look how godless the world has become. Well, as bad as things were then and are now, apparently they weren't and aren't bad enough yet. Paul points to two major events that must occur.

First, notice that word *rebellion* in verse 3. That's the Greek word *apostasia* from which we get the English word *apostasy*. It means "a massive revolt, a departure, and an abandoning of a position that was once held." It refers to an *en masse* leaving of the faith within "professing churches." This is not just a general coldness but an actual, deliberate turning away from God and from His Word. Second Thessalonians 2:5 tells us that Paul had discussed this with them in person. He asks, "Do you not remember that when I was still with you I told you these things?" Isn't that a teaching session we would have enjoyed sitting in on? Fortunately, this apostasy, this deliberate turning away, is discussed elsewhere in Scripture (see, for example, 1 Tim. 4:1; 2 Tim. 3:1–9, 4:3–4 and 2 Pet. 2:1–22).

The second development leading to the day of the Lord, wrote Paul, is when "the man of lawlessness is revealed, the son of destruction" (2 Thess. 2:3). Now, who is this man of sin? He's a leader on the world stage. He makes a covenant with Israel at the beginning of the seventieth week of Daniel (Dan. 9:27). And when he gets to the middle of that time three-and-a-half years later, he breaks that covenant. This is the Antichrist. This is the man who opposes God; who sets himself up as God (see 2 Thess. 2:4). Could these things be ready to unfold today? They could be, just as they could have been in Paul's day. We don't know; we wait. But we do know this: before the great and terrible day of the Lord there will be a falling away, an apostasy from the faith. The Church will lose millions of people. And the Antichrist will arise as a world leader. Until you see those two things happen, the end isn't yet.

The Thessalonians were confused. They thought they'd missed the Lord's Rapture. They were expecting nothing but bad times ahead. We've seen a similar kind of confusion in our lifetime. We've heard about (or known) people so sure the end was about to come that they stopped waiting and began saying things Scripture forbids such as, "I know He's coming the day after tomorrow." So Paul wrote his little second letter to tell them, "When the great and terrible day of the Lord comes, when the Lord comes back in power and great glory, when He comes back with His heavenly armies, when He rides out of heaven on a white horse, you'll know!"

Those who are waiting for the Lord, intent on living by His Word, don't have to worry about missing being "caught up" to heaven. Paul's two letters are filled with *in the meantime* activities we can do while waiting. The waiting is always easier when we're busy, but we can't forget we're waiting and anticipating at the same time. We must be on guard against joining in apostasy or minimizing God's Word. Paul's closing thoughts in this chapter (vv. 13–17) can be as present and continuous a comfort as they must have been to those anxious Macedonians long ago.

Express It

As you prepare to pray, consider that believers through the years and even today have suffered and died for Christ. Yet the day of the Lord will be terrible. It will be the end of Creation and the start of a new one. Those who are not in Christ will not survive. Living and waiting for Christ doesn't mean an easy road, but we can be thankful for His presence every day. And we can pray continually for those we know who have not yet trusted Christ as Savior. We want them with Christ and with us on the great and terrible day of the Lord.

Consider It

As you read 2 Thessalonians 2:1–17, consider these questions:

1) Why is it crucial to distinguish between "being gathered together" (v. 1) with the Lord and experiencing the "day of the Lord" (v. 2)?

_____

_____

_____

2) What kind of person will the "man of lawlessness" be, and have there been any candidates in history that might have led to the conclusion that "the day of the Lord" was approaching?

_____

_____

_____

3) How would you explain and illustrate the word "rebellion"? (See v. 3.)

_____

_____

_____

4) What is Satan's role during the events leading up to the day of the Lord?

_____

_____

_____

5) What points of confidence can Christians remember as we wait for Christ?

_____

_____

_____

6) What do you think active waiting involves? In what ways is your life an example of active waiting?

_____

_____

_____

7) In verses 13–17, what reasons to stand firm can you find?

_____

_____

Busy, not Busybodies

After a program we're watching on television is interrupted by a special report, we're used to hearing the announcement, "And now, back to our regularly scheduled programming." Trusting and waiting for Jesus feels like our regularly scheduled programming. Should it?

2 Thessalonians 3:1–18

Pray for Us

3 Finally, brothers, pray for us, that the word of the Lord may speed ahead and be honored, as happened among you, ²and that we may be delivered from wicked and evil men. For not all have faith. ³But the Lord is faithful. He will establish you and guard you against the evil one. ⁴And we have confidence in the Lord about you, that you are doing and will do the things that we command. ⁵May the Lord direct your hearts to the love of God and to the steadfastness of Christ.

Warning Against Idleness

⁶Now we command you, brothers, in the name of our Lord Jesus Christ, that you keep away from any brother who is walking in idleness and not in accord with the tradition that you received from us. ⁷For you yourselves know how you ought to imitate us, because we were not idle when we were with you, ⁸nor did we eat anyone's bread without paying for it, but with toil and labor we worked night and day, that we might not be a burden to any of you. ⁹It was not because we do not have that right, but to give you in ourselves an example to imitate. ¹⁰For even when we were with you, we would give you this command:

If anyone is not willing to work, let him not eat. ¹¹For we hear that some among you walk in idleness, not busy at work, but busybodies. ¹²Now such persons we command and encourage in the Lord Jesus Christ to do their work quietly and to earn their own living.

¹³As for you, brothers, do not grow weary in doing good. ¹⁴If anyone does not obey what we say in this letter, take note of that person, and have nothing to do with him, that he may be ashamed. ¹⁵Do not regard him as an enemy, but warn him as a brother.

Benediction

¹⁶Now may the Lord of peace himself give you peace at all times in every way. The Lord be with you all.

¹⁷I, Paul, write this greeting with my own hand. This is the sign of genuineness in every letter of mine; it is the way I write. ¹⁸The grace of our Lord Jesus Christ be with you all.

Key Verse

"As for you, brothers, do not grow weary in doing good" (2 Thess. 3:13).

Go Deeper

Besides the Parable of the Ten Virgins, Jesus told two others that parallel the practical teaching Paul gave to the Thessalonians: The Parable of the Traveling Owner (Mark 13:34–37) and the Parable of the Wise and Foolish Servants (Matt. 24:45–51; Luke 12:42–48). Several themes can be seen in each of these stories. The unexpected return of the central character was Jesus' main point, but the state of those he surprised holds a good point of application for us.

(continued)

Go Deeper Continued . . .

Everyone in these parables is surprised, but the surprise turns out well for some and not so well for others.

Before the Parable of the Traveling Owner, Jesus briefly explained His meaning: "Be on guard, keep awake. For you do not know when the time will come" (Mark 13:33). A man goes on a journey and leaves his servants to tend his home and await his return. He is not required to tell them ahead of time when he will come back. He expects them to be ready for him at any time. What would displease the master is to find his servants asleep. This is not about Jesus forbidding His disciples from getting a good night's sleep. If the house, the servants, and the duties are metaphorical, so is the sleep. We are not to be sleepwalking or sleep-living when Jesus returns. He expects us rested, healthy and busy for Him—never busybodies.

The Parable of the Wise and Foolish Servants (Luke 12:42–48) has a similar point with different details. Here the servant isn't sleeping but busy doing wrong. The servant assumes the delay means the master will not come anytime soon. But just because the Master hasn't returned doesn't mean the Master is oblivious to the servant's actions. Being caught by the Lord doing nothing or doing evil will lead to an unhappy ending. There's only one way to fix this: "Do not be deceived: God is not mocked, for whatever one sows, that will he also reap. For the one who sows to his own flesh will from the flesh reap corruption, but the one who sows to the Spirit will from the Spirit reap eternal life. And let us not grow weary of doing good, for in due season we will reap, if we do not give up" (Gal. 6:7–9).

Paul's first letter to the Thessalonians closed with a simple request, "Brothers, pray for us" (1 Thess. 5:25). He began that letter with prayer for them and ended by expressing his need for prayer from them. This is a pattern he maintained in almost all his letters. In this second letter, Paul made the same request, but he gave them some direction about how to pray. He wanted them to pray for his message and his mission—that the message they had heard from him would have the same effect in new places, and that he and his team would be protected from their adversaries.

After that pause for prayer, Paul again plunged into the specifics of the active waiting aspects of the Christian life. He reminded them we live and move in a world where "not all have faith" (2 Thess. 3:2), which makes it all the more important that we never lose sight of the fact that "the Lord is faithful" (v. 3). Verses 3–5 form a brief description of Paul's confidence in God concerning the Thessalonians. Ultimately, Paul knew his friends were in God's care.

From verses 6 to 15, Paul takes care of what we might call spiritual house rules. The love he expected the Thessalonians to shower on one another needed to be tempered with a toughness that emphasized personal responsibility. Believers were not to presume on one another's generosity. Paul pointed to his own example among them. He had not taken advantage of them. He hadn't been idle, nor had he eaten "anyone's bread without paying for it, but with toil and labor we worked night and day, that we might not be a burden to any of you" (v. 8). Verse 9 tells us he knew he could have expected their hospitality and support in response to his work of sharing the Gospel and teaching them, but he wanted to give them an example.

Based on his example Paul could say, "For even when we were with you, we would give you this command: If anyone is not willing to work, let him not eat" (v. 10). This may sound harsh at first, but Paul is not talking about ability here. Someone who is genuinely unable to work should not be allowed to go hungry, and such are the situations that allow believers to meet one another's needs. In 2 Thessalonians 3:10 Paul is addressing a problem. He had heard that there were some who were acting like parasites on the Body of Christ. They were taking at will without making any contribution to the whole. In the context of this letter, they could have been people who thought the coming of the Lord was so close that they could coast in every way. Paul firmly confronted and condemned that attitude of entitlement. Waiting expectantly for Christ didn't mean not working in the meantime!

So how do we wait for the coming of the Lord to receive us to Himself? First of all, we keep busy for the Lord. We don't sell our house and go to a mountaintop to sit cross-legged in meditation. We don't join a little club someplace, where there are only 60 members and hole up expecting to disappear one day. That's not God's plan. That's not a healthy way to live in expectation of what Christ will do at the proper time. Paul clearly says in verses 10–12, "Get a job; contribute in the work force; get back in the church; get back to doing what you always did." Then he says to those who hadn't given up their jobs, "As for you, brothers, do not grow weary in doing good" (v. 13). In other words, "Hang in there. Keep watching and working because, after all, either the Lord will come back and take us to Himself, or, after whatever time the Lord has allotted to us, we will be taken from this life and meet Him in the air."

Verse 11 includes a great little play on words that can give us a guiding motto: busy at work, not busybodies; busy doing what God wants us to do, not busy doing nothing or what the Lord doesn't want us to do. Jesus told a parable about ten virgins who were excitedly waiting for the bridegroom to arrive (Matt. 25:1–13). But five of them were prepared for the wait and brought extra oil while the other five ran out. When the shortsighted rushed to try to find more oil, the bridegroom arrived, and they missed him. Foresight and added labor by the five wise virgins were required in order to keep their lamps lit for the groom's arrival. Jesus summarized that parable with this statement: "Watch therefore, for you know neither the day nor the hour" (Matt. 25:13). The apostle Paul gave the Thessalonians and us his own version of that same message. We don't want to become weary doing the good it takes to keep the supply of oil in the lamp so that the world can see our light!

Express It

Prayer is certainly part of active waiting. It keeps the line of communication open between God and us. He speaks continuously through His Word and His Spirit in us. Our responses are somewhat less constant, but they can always improve. Take some time to talk to God about your feelings and struggles as you wait for His return.

Consider It

As you read 2 Thessalonians 3:1–18, consider these questions:

1) Which of Paul's two prayer requests strikes you as the most personal? Why?

_____

_____

2) What does Paul trust God to do to maintain the safety of the Thessalonians?

_____

_____

3) What are the command and the conditions that Paul lays down about the treatment of those who are "walking in idleness" (v. 6)?

_____

_____

4) How would you describe Paul's idea of a healthy community of believers?

_____

_____

5) Why was it important for Paul to set a high standard of personal behavior when he was with the Thessalonians?

_____

_____

6) How does this chapter challenge some of your assumptions and philosophy about work and relating to other Christians?

_____

_____

7) What effect does Paul's closing benediction (vv. 16–18) create in you as you think of him writing this to someone like you?

_____

_____

Lesson **10**

Summary Lesson: Constant Companion

Is it possible to trust until Christ returns? It certainly is. But we need help along the way. In fact, being aware of the resources God makes available to us increases the likelihood that we will be alert and waiting when He returns.

1 Thessalonians 4:13–18

The Coming of the Lord

¹³But we do not want you to be uninformed, brothers, about those who are asleep, that you may not grieve as others do who have no hope. ¹⁴For since we believe that Jesus died and rose again, even so, through Jesus, God will bring with him those who have fallen asleep. ¹⁵For this we declare to you by a word from the Lord, that we who are alive, who are left until the coming of the Lord, will not precede those who have fallen asleep. ¹⁶For the Lord himself will descend from heaven with a cry of command, with the voice of an archangel, and with the sound of the trumpet of God. And the dead in Christ will rise first. ¹⁷Then we who are alive, who are left, will be caught up together with them in the clouds to meet the Lord in the air, and so we will always be with the Lord. ¹⁸Therefore encourage one another with these words.

Key Verse

For since we believe that Jesus died and rose again, even so, through Jesus, God will bring with him those who have fallen asleep (1 Thess. 4:14). *To this he called you through our gospel, so that you may obtain the glory of our Lord Jesus Christ* (2 Thess. 2:14).

Go Deeper

Paul wrote these two letters with glowing feelings about the progress of the Thessalonians. They had come a long way spiritually in a very short time against significant resistance. He wanted to commend their faith as well as urge it on. He wanted to acknowledge their difficulties without making them feel like victims. He wanted to assure them that they were not in the struggle alone. And he wanted to give them confidence in God that they could trust Jesus until He comes—even if He didn't come in their lifetime.

His affirming references to their faith can be found in 1 Thessalonians 1:3, 8; 3:2, 6–7 and 2 Thessalonians 1:3–4. He acknowledged their afflictions

in 1 Thessalonians 1:6; 3:4, 7 and 2 Thessalonians 1:4, 5, 6. And he strengthened their connection with God's peace in 1 Thessalonians 1:1; 5:23 and 2 Thessalonians 1:2; 3:16. Paul knew his brethren in Thessalonica faced many obstacles, including the difficulty of waiting, but he also knew there was great help from God available for the journey.

That's why Paul could say, after describing how Christ will handle those who are alive and those who have died when he comes for the Church, "Therefore encourage one another with these words" (1 Thess. 4:18). His words apply to us too. Be encouraged and trust Him until He returns. He will. He promised.

These two letters from Paul tell us a lot about his audience, but they also tell us a lot about him. He continued to care deeply about people after he had passed along the message Christ entrusted to him. He sought to find out how they were doing. In this case, when he had to leave the young church long before he wanted to, he sent Timothy back to get an eyewitness report on its spiritual welfare. He perked up every time he heard news about how they were doing. And he was thrilled with their progress and let them know it! Even though he was far from them most of the time, they must have felt that Paul was a constant, although distant, companion.

In all, Paul visited this church three times and wrote them at least these two letters. His visits were always short. The apostle mentions frequently the afflictions (1 Thess. 1:6; 3:3; 2 Thess. 1:4, 7) faced by those young believers and his delight over their endurance. He may well have been torn over the effects of his visits, because while he got to encourage them, it is also likely that opposition and persecution increased for them when Paul was around. Acts 20:1–6 contains most of what we know about Paul's two visits after the founding one. They came within six months of each other. As usual, Paul was on his way to or from a riot. He left Ephesus after staying two years and three months building the church (Acts 19:1–20). At that point, Paul sent Timothy and Erastus ahead of him into Macedonia (Acts 19:21–22). They undoubtedly visited Thessalonica. Shortly after they left, a fierce backlash developed in Ephesus, and Paul had to leave the area. He journeyed through Philippi, Thessalonica, and Berea on his way to Greece and then reversed that itinerary several months later. Each time he confirmed the message he had recorded in his letters.

Paul was an urgent man. He had an urgent message and there was a large world to which he planned to deliver it. He was applying literally the Great Commission and traveling to take the Gospel to the ends of the earth. As far as he knew, the events leading to the end of the world might well happen in his own lifetime. No wonder he was so intense! No wonder he had to follow up his spread of the Gospel with teaching that emphasized that discipleship and trust in Christ weren't short-term responses; they had to be long-term resolves.

"It turns out that Jesus is our present companion along the way until He returns. He promised to be with us until the very moment that we are with Him in glory! Now, that's good news."

The Holy Spirit gave Paul two huge markers in God's plan to pass on to others: (1) Christ's removal of the believers from the world, the Rapture—"And the dead in Christ will rise first. Then we who are alive, who are left, will be caught up together with them in the clouds to meet the Lord in the air, and so we will always be with the Lord" (1 Thess. 4:16–17); and (2) the day of the Lord—"For you yourselves are fully aware that the day of the Lord will come like a thief in the night" (1 Thess. 5:2). The day of the Lord (see Go Deeper in Lesson 8) would arrive by surprise, and the effects would be devastating. It would involve a general rebellion against the teachings of God's Word (called the "falling away" in the NKJV) and the rise of the Antichrist (2 Thess. 2:3). This then would lead to the second coming of Jesus in glory and power (2 Thess. 2:8).

Paul's letters served as a constant reminder that, though the end was determined, getting to it might take a while. Yes, believers would die before Christ's return, but that wouldn't be a problem. The biggest problem would be living as faithful disciples during the waiting time before Christ returns. The letters were like a travel guide for the journey to be consulted for directions along the way. In that way, they were and are a constant companion (as is all of God's Word).

In Matthew's account, Jesus' final words stress the reality of another constant companion: "And behold, I am with you always, to the end of the age" (Matt. 28:20). Paul closed both these letters to the Thessalonians with the same statement: "The grace of our Lord Jesus Christ be with you" (1 Thess. 5:28; 2 Thess. 3:18). He added "all" to the sign-off of the second letter. How do we know Christ is with us? One way we know is by the presence of His grace. Not only are we saved by His grace through faith (Eph. 2:8), but we also need His gracious presence every step of the way until He comes. Paul understood and helps us understand that we can count on that help. He encouraged his readers in each letter: "He who calls you is faithful; he will surely do it" (1 Thess. 5:24); "But the Lord is faithful. He will establish you and guard you against the evil one" (2 Thess. 3:3). It turns out that Jesus is our present companion along the way until He returns. He promised to be with us until the very moment that we are with Him in glory! Now, that's good news.

Express It

As you pray, consider how far you have come in your journey following Jesus. If you haven't started, trust Him today. If you have been following Jesus for a little while or for decades, thank Him for His faithfulness. Put into words your desire to trust Him for every step along the way until He comes.

Consider It

As you review 1 & 2 Thessalonians, consider these questions:

1) What people in your life have had a Paul-like impact on you? Whose visits and letters have always made a significant difference? How have they done that?

_____

_____

_____

2) What have you learned in this study about perseverance?

_____

_____

3) When you think about your own journey with Christ, how would you describe your level of long-term trust?

_____

_____

_____

4) In what ways did you feel companionship with Paul as you studied these letters?

_____

_____

_____

5) How and when do you sense Christ being "with you always, to the end of the age" (Matt. 28:20)?

_____

_____

_____

6) We know the *who, what, where,* and *how* of God's plan for the end times. Why do you suppose He hasn't told us the *when*?

_____

_____

_____

7) What question(s) has been answered for you by this study of 1 & 2 Thessalonians?

_____

_____

_____

Notes

Notes

Notes

Notes

Notes

Notes